SandCastle 3

Do You Wonder?

What?

Mary Elizabeth Salzmann

ABDO
Publishing Company

Published by SandCastle™, an imprint of ABDO Publishing Company, 4940 Viking Drive, Edina, Minnesota 55435.

Printed in the United States.

Photo credits: Adobe, Comstock, Corel, PhotoDisc

Library of Congress Cataloging-in-Publication Data

Salzmann, Mary Elizabeth, 1968-
    What? / Mary Elizabeth Salzmann.
      p. cm. -- (Do you wonder?)
    Summary: Simple questions and answers about people and things, using the word "what."
    ISBN 1-57765-170-7 (alk. paper) -- ISBN 1-57765-281-9 (set)
      1. Readers (Primary) 2. Readers--Children's questions and answers. [1. Readers. 2. Questions and answers.] I. Title.

PE1119 .S2347 2000
428.1--dc21

                                                                     99-046484

The SandCastle concept, content, and reading method have been reviewed and approved by a national advisory board including literacy specialists, librarians, elementary school teachers, early childhood education professionals, and parents.

Let Us Know

After reading the book, SandCastle would like you to tell us your stories about reading. What is your favorite page? Was there something hard that you needed help with? Share the ups and downs of learning to read. We want to hear from you! To get posted on the Abdo Publishing Company Web site, send us email at:

sandcastle@abdopub.com

About SandCastle™
Nonfiction books for the beginning reader

- Basic concepts of phonics are incorporated with integrated language methods of reading instruction. Most words are short, and phrases, letter sounds, and word sounds are repeated.

- Readability is determined by the number of words in each sentence, the number of characters in each word, and word lists based on curriculum frameworks.

- Full-color photography reinforces word meanings and concepts.

- "Words I Can Read" list at the end of each book teaches basic elements of grammar, helps the reader recognize the words in the text, and builds vocabulary.

- Reading levels are indicated by the number of flags on the castle.

Look for more SandCastle books in these three reading levels:

Level 1 (one flag)	Level 2 (two flags)	Level 3 (three flags)

Grades Pre-K to K 5 or fewer words per page	**Grades K to 1** 5 to 10 words per page	**Grades 1 to 2** 10 to 15 words per page

I use the word **what** to ask questions about persons or things.

What am I kicking?

I am kicking a soccer ball.

What are we playing?

We are playing tug-of-war.

What am I painting?

I am painting an orange dinosaur.

What are Dad and I washing?

Dad and I are washing our car.

What am I wearing on my head?

I am wearing a crown made of flowers.

What am I swinging on?

I am swinging on a tire swing.

What am I holding?

I am holding my new puppy.

What sleeps with me?

Three stuffed monkeys sleep with me.

Words I Can Read

Nouns

A noun is a person, place, or thing

car (KAR) p. 13
crown (KROUN) p. 15
Dad (DAD) p. 13
dinosaur (DYE-nuh-sor)
  p. 11
head (HED) p. 15
puppy (PUHP-ee) p. 19

soccer ball
  (SOK-ur BAWL) p. 7
tire swing (TIRE SWING)
  p. 17
tug-of-war
  (TUHG-UHV-WOR) p. 9
word (WURD) p. 5

Plural Nouns

A plural noun is more than one
person, place, or thing

flowers (FLOU-urz) p. 15
monkeys (MUHNG-keez)
  p. 21
persons (PUR-suhnz) p. 5

questions
  (KWESS-chuhnz) p. 5
things (THINGZ) p. 5

Pronouns

A pronoun is a word that replaces a noun

I (EYE) pp. 5, 7, 11, 13, 15,
  17, 19
me (MEE) p. 21

we (WEE) p. 9
what (WOT) pp. 5, 7, 9, 11,
  13, 15, 17, 19, 21

22

Verbs

A verb is an action or being word

am (AM) pp. 7, 11, 15, 17, 19
are (AR) pp. 9, 11, 13
ask (ASK) p. 5
holding (HOHLD-ing) p. 19
kicking (KIK-ing) p. 7
made (MADE) p. 15
painting (PAYNT-ing) p. 11
playing (PLAY-ing) p. 9

sleep (SLEEP) p. 21
sleeps (SLEEPS) p. 21
swinging (SWING-ing) p. 17
use (YOOZ) p. 5
washing (WOSH-ing) p. 13
wearing (WAIR-ing) p. 15

Adjectives

An adjective describes something

my (MYE) pp. 15, 19
new (NOO) p. 19
orange (OR-inj) p. 11

our (OUR) p. 13
stuffed (STUHFT) p. 21
three (THREE) p. 21

23

Glossary

crown – a head covering often worn by a king or queen.

dinosaur – a type of reptile that lived long ago.

head – the top part of your body where your brain and face are.

monkeys – small, ape-like animals, often with long tails.

puppy – a young dog.

tug-of-war – a game between two teams that pull on opposite ends of a rope until one team is pulled across a center line.